MW01295701

the
ST. BERNARD
PRINCIPLE

Why Specialists are the Alpha Dogs in Business.

by Paul J. Welsh

Dedicated to all of my partners over the years, especially my life partner, my wife Neicey.

CONTENTS

Introduction

Every dog lover has a favorite. Any choice is fine
when you're just looking for a companion. But
as business people, our customers usually have
needs beyond companionship. (Pet stores and
dating services notwithstanding.)

So let's suppose you are a European trader. You
begin interviewing dogs to help you travel back and
forth across the Alps between Switzerland and Italy
recognizing how treacherous the winters can be. You'll
want a specialist. You'll ask questions like, "Do you have
any experience helping people cross the Alps?" "Is this
a specialty of yours?" Those are the kinds of questions
your prospects ask you. And they make decisions largely
on your specific answers.

In this case, the St. Bernard is well positioned to get
your business. He reminds you that in the 1700's, St.
Bernard dogs were used to rescue people trapped in
the frigid Alpine wilderness. Their dense coats protect
them from the biting cold allowing them to function
outside for extended periods. Plus, they have a keen
instinct for predicting snowstorms and avalanches.
What's more, their spectacular sense of direction helps

when driving snowstorms reduce vision. As a specialist, the St. Bernard can rattle off abundant selling points to differentiate his business from the Poodles, Rottweilers and Golden Retrievers. How could you not give him your business?

So how do you become a successful St. Bernard in your industry?

This book will show you how to identify and promote a specialty. A specialist position will set you apart from your competition and help you grow your business in ways no generalist can.

Whether you're a small to mid-sized business that's been around for years or an entrepreneur preparing to launch your business, the St. Bernard Principle is worth considering. It's an opportunity to position your business as a specialist and leave generalists back in the pack.

Chapter One
The Case for Specialization.

The Case for Specialization.

The specialist versus generalist argument has been hotly contested for generations with good arguments on both sides. However, when you measure risk against reward, the most compelling arguments I've found, and experienced, fall on the side of the specialist.

To be a St. Bernard you have to position yourself based on your special strengths and use them to create differentiation. You don't claim to be a speed merchant when you're competing with a Greyhound. And you probably don't want to audition for a Taco Bell commercial if you're up against a Chihuahua.

Generalists claim to be good at everything. But nobody believes any business can do everything at a high level. If you're honest with yourself, you know that's true. More to the point, that's not what customers want to buy anyway. They want to know that you have special skills and experience to satisfy their specific needs in their "unique" industry. (No matter how mundane, every business owner thinks their industry is somehow unique.) When you find a specialty and promote it, you have a much greater chance of selling your product or service.

When my youngest brother had colon cancer, any surgeon could have cut 21 inches out of his colon; but he chose a colorectal surgeon. Why? It was important to him, so he picked a "specialist."

Specialization is treasured in every aspect of the business world, not just the medical profession.

In my marketing practice, almost every prospect I call on asks me these two questions:

"Have you ever done any work in my industry?"

"What do you specialize in?"

Those two questions are telling. Experience and specialization are important to prospects and customers. If you've ever been asked those questions, and you probably have, you know people prefer specialists.

"Generalists claim to be good at everything. But nobody believes any business can do everything at a high level."

the
ST. BERNARD
PRINCIPLE

Prospects don't care if you've starred in a Taco Bell commercial if they need to be rescued from an Alps pass full of snowdrifts. A brandy keg around the neck of a Chihuahua lacks credibility.

Short of being referred by somebody your prospect  knows, there's nothing more important to them than your experience in their industry.

Rebutting the Generalists
Generalists argue that specialization is risky and limits opportunities by painting you into a corner. Maybe that went through the minds of Henry and Richard Bloch when they decided to specialize in personal tax returns. You can imagine naysayers speculating on how foolish it is to have a business that essentially shuts down after April 15 every year. Yet choosing specialization has worked for them. H&R Block has been in business for more than 50 years. In 2009 they had $4.1 billion in total revenues with 13,000 tax offices serving 24 million tax clients. If that's being painted into a corner, bring on the paint. It's a great example of a company that had a specialist strategy from the very beginning.

But what about a business that is already operating as a generalist? How can they afford to change when their established customer base is diverse? That's one of the biggest drawbacks I hear from existing businesses when they think about moving to a specialist position. But the upsides can make it more than worthwhile.

A high-profile example would be Frederick Smith with Federal Express. When he decided to focus on overnight delivery, moving away from his generalist model, the business took off. Of course, to own that position FedEx needed to deliver on their promise and they did. In all the years I've been in business I can never remember a single overnight FedEx package that didn't arrive on time. In 2009, FedEx revenues were $35.5 billion. They didn't achieve that by being positioned as a generalist. In the same way, specialization can help your business seize opportunities that otherwise wouldn't exist in any meaningful way.

But this book is not about jumbo corporations as they exist now, but more about how small and mid-sized businesses can use specialization to get bigger and more profitable. It's about entrepreneurs who wonder if specialization might give their businesses a leg up. Maybe even help them become a jumbo corporation someday if that's their goal.

Specialists don't beat generalists every time but in head-to-head matchups they win most of the time. That's because all things considered, most of us prefer a specialist.

Specialists and the POOCH Factors

Specialization is one "doggone" good way to position your business for success. And you'll see why as you compare generalists and specialists using my business development **POOCH** Factors:

P—Psychological leverage (Chapter Two)
O—Open doors (Chapter Three)
O—Outflank competition (Chapter Four)
C—Cost-efficient marketing (Chapter Five)
H—Home and away opportunities (Chapter Six)

TAKEAWAY POINT:
Buyers prefer specialists.

Chapter Two
Psychological Leverage.

the
ST. BERNARD
PRINCIPLE

Psychological Leverage.

Purchasing decisions are closely tied to cognition and there are a number of psychological principles that favor specialists.

Cognitive Dissonance.
Cognitive psychologists will tell you that humans can't hold two conflicting beliefs at the same time. If you believe the Beatles were the best rock combo ever then your mind won't let you believe it's the Rolling Stones. Similarly, if you are perceived as the leader in any specialty area, it's almost impossible for any competitor, especially a generalist, to change that person's belief.

Once a European trader decides the St. Bernard is his best choice for crossing the Alps, it becomes much more difficult for a German Shepherd to claim Crossing-the-Alps leadership. With apologies to the magnificent exploits of Rin Tin Tin, the St. Bernard already owns that position.

Confirmation Bias.
Many psychologists suggest that this lack of willingness to change one's mind about product and service preferences is tied to people's personal biases. One example is "confirmation bias." That's a tendency to confirm what we believe and discount what we don't.

We tend to have selective recall and recognize things that support our point of view while ignoring what is contradictory. To do otherwise would be to admit we're wrong and not many of us are blessed with that ability.

For example, if we believe American cars are less dependable than Japanese cars we'll see the Malibu broken down on the side of the road. But we'll totally overlook the Camry being towed five miles back. We search for information that confirms our preconceptions. This can lead to bad consumer decisions on occasion but it's only a positive if that preference favors your product or service. Indeed, perception is reality and specialization helps feed a positive perception.

Distinction Bias.

"Distinction bias" is the tendency to view the differences between two options as more extreme when evaluating them at the same time as opposed to evaluating them separately.

Over the years I've worked with a lot of sales people who have stated their preference for a negotiated sale. That's where you pitch your product or service without a competitor in the picture. Sales people inherently know that when they're being evaluated "separately" acceptance comes easier.

Since the prospect is not viewing you and a competitor side by side, the differences are not as pronounced. Essentially you're being judged on your own merits. The selling points you can make as a specialist can give the prospect confidence to buy from you without comparing you with someone else.

Being a specialist also works well when your prospect is viewing you simultaneously with another option. All the benefits you present become even more extreme. Presenting separately an Alaskan Husky could make a good case to a European trader who wants to cross the Alps. But side by side with a St. Bernard, the Husky's capabilities seem very limited.

Whether you're being compared to others or being evaluated on your own merits, specialization helps you come out on the right side of distinction bias. That's because you have substantive differences to highlight.

Differentiation versus imitation
Specialists by their nature embrace differentiation over imitation. When a business can't or doesn't differentiate, they lose opportunities.

I was helping a general contractor client develop messaging for their new website. They totally understood that they weren't in a position to compete with the #1 general contractor in town. They told me so. But they went on to say they were very attractive and competitive within certain business segments.

With that input, the first draft copy for their website was written to target those audiences that they were best equipped to serve. However, upon reading that first draft they rejected it. Instead, they requested a website message similar to what the #1 general contractor presented on their website. This smaller general contractor's new website is nice and parallels the industry leader, but it does little to communicate a true competitive advantage. It misses the opportunity to connect with the prospects who are most likely to become their satisfied customers. That's the equivalent of a **Great Dane trying to position itself as a lap dog. Not on my lap!**

Sameness is expensive.

It's amazing to me how many companies mimic their competitors. Yet sameness is the basis for commodity selling. And when you're selling commodities, price is almost always the sales determinant. So if you're interested in reduced margins, focus on imitation. But when the goal is increased margins look to product differentiation opportunities like specialization.

The smaller their market share the more open companies are to present themselves as different. They think, "If we're seventh in the market maybe we need to leave our comfort zone and not look like our competitors." At one point I had a bank client who was exactly in that place. We presented an advertising campaign for home mortgages that was very different than typical bank advertising. They agreed to try it.

As we were leaving their conference room the Senior Vice President said to me, "I think this campaign will work." I asked him why he thought so. He answered, "The President doesn't like it and neither do I."

Were it not for their low market share, the bank would not have been willing to walk away from their bias against being different. By changing, they not only escaped their bias, but they helped their prospects work through their own distinction biases. That year the bank's mortgage business increased by more than 400% with an advertising budget similar to the previous year. The success was chronicled in a story that appeared in *Bank Marketing* magazine.

TAKEAWAY POINT:
Cognitive psychology
favors specialists.

Chapter Three
Specialization Opens Doors.

Specialization Opens Doors.

When you're a generalist, your prospect pool is larger but so is your competitor pool. Without a defined position you're just a dog, but positioned as a specialist, you're a mighty St. Bernard. Specialization creates a doggie door that gives you easier access to prospects and here's why.

Most prospects already have preferred suppliers and are not eager to meet with businesses that appear to offer similar products and services. That's not to say that they don't accept sales calls but most do so reluctantly. They believe sales pitches from new companies are time consuming and unproductive if they're happy with the folks they're already using. Companies view those meetings as something to file away in case they get unhappy with their current arrangements at a later date. Plus, they can easily become overwhelmed by the number of people saying "Buy my product!" knowing they don't have time to see everyone. So who gets their ear? Who gets a face-to-face meeting? All else being equal, it's the St. Bernard.

A St. Bernard has a better opportunity to get an appointment because he has a simpler and more appealing story to tell. One that appears different from what the prospect is currently buying. So even before the sales call the St. Bernard has been differentiated from its generalist competitors. If nothing else, the prospects are more likely to be good listeners when specialists get sales appointments.

Specialization in phases

One of my clients in the direct marketing industry was
a generalist selling to both for-profit businesses and non-
profits. Appointment setting was brutal because most
companies they called on were reasonably comfortable
with their vendors and not looking to change.
The prospects saw little benefit in accepting a sales call
from new vendors that didn't seem any different than
those they were using.

My client was a generalist, and although they saw the
benefits of specialization they were admittedly fearful
about taking the plunge. That's because they were
hesitant to reduce their overall prospect base. So they
decided to ease in to St. Bernard status.

Their first step toward specialization was to focus a
majority of their sales calls on the non-profit sector. Any
business will make X number of sales calls so focusing
calls on your specialty segment is a simple and logical
first step. They weren't a St. Bernard right off the bat
but looking like a Newfoundland was a sign of progress.
However, just concentrating on non-profits didn't open
the doors as easily as they had hoped. Even when they
did get appointments it was as if they were being tossed a
bone that rarely had any meat on it.

So my client began to look more seriously at the St. Bernard Principle. This drove them to do significant investigation online, in print and in conversations to find out if there was a category that wasn't being served. Ideally, if such a category existed there would be less competition and more prospect enthusiasm for their message. Find that, they reasoned, and doors would open. That's exactly what happened.

The gem they found was related to monthly giving. That category had the potential to ease the stress on non-profits, most of whom face inconsistent cash flow. The reality was that traditional fundraising success was tied to one-time contributions through individual events or solicitations. With that model, erratic cash flow was predictable. Some non-profits had dabbled into monthly giving with minimal success. Most often it was little more than a check-box option on their existing mailings.

Armed with that knowledge, my direct marketing client dug into books and websites to see if any fundraising companies had established leadership in this desirable segment. A few people had published articles and books on the topic of monthly giving. But, most writings were dated and nobody seemed to be focusing on monthly giving as a specialty. It was good news for my client because the potential seemed tremendous and competitors appeared content to be generalists. Once my client identified this opportunity they consumed everything they could find on the monthly giving category. They began developing fresh strategies that focused less on monthly giving and more on monthly givers. That led to developing tactics to build relationships with givers. In the process they created an entirely new fundraising category called "Monthly Engaged Giving."

Almost immediately the doors at non-profits became easier to open. It didn't guarantee sales but this specialist message made it easier to get in front of prospects and separated my client from their competitors. What's more, prospects were eager to hear what they had to say because it was something different. And it addressed the cash flow pain point. No longer was my client an annoying mutt, they were a lovable St. Bernard.

The story repeats itself.
Here are a couple of similar examples.
1. A major independent ad agency I co-founded produced about a dozen quarterly newsletters a year. It was a small percent of our revenues but a nice piece of income nonetheless. There was another company in town that positioned themselves as "newsletter specialists." Nearly every time my agency had the opportunity to pitch a new newsletter assignment this

"We would have preferred that the St. Bernard would quit showing up in our yard."

newsletter specialist company was also in the pitch. In the dog-eat-dog agency business we constantly were facing this St. Bernard. We won sometimes and lost other times but that much smaller specialist company was always in the running. When we beat them it was usually based on a strong existing relationship.
We would have preferred that the St. Bernard would quit showing up in our yard.

Since all that company did was newsletters, and they promoted that distinction well, they got constant referrals wherever newsletters were involved. I asked one of the owners of that company if their clients ever asked them to do more than newsletters. She told me that they had frequent requests to do brochures or advertising. In most cases, however, they turned down those requests to prevent diluting their specialist position and brand. When they did accept non-newsletter work they didn't talk much about it. In fact, they intentionally kept it quiet.

2. Another past client of mine was a very good architectural firm who was definitely a generalist.

They did historic preservation work, residential work, commercial structures and hospital operating suites to name a few. After getting to the finals but losing a major dormitory project for a University, they were told they never had a chance. That's because, the University said, they were a boutique firm (another name for generalist).

Shortly after that, they began to focus on radiology, nuclear medicine and **MRI** Suite design and consulting. They set up a separate division for that specialty and are a major player nationally. They figured this out by themselves without any help from me. In fact, their success was one of the examples that got me looking into the role of specialization in business success. Now they speak at conferences, help establish industry standards and have developed an electronic newsletter devoted to their specialty.

TAKEAWAY POINT:
Specialization makes opening doors easier and fosters improved listening skills in prospects.

Chapter Four
Outflank Generalists for a Competitive Edge.

Outflank Generalists for a Competitive Edge.

When you are a generalist, your list of competitors is naturally larger as I mentioned in Chapter Three. So just based on sheer numbers of competitors, being a generalist is a tough position to be in. The reality is, when you're up against specialists you better be a terrific sales person if you expect to be top dog competing against their resumé.

Here's just one example of why I say that.

Several years ago one of the consulting services I offered was "advertising agency search." For one assignment I was helping a healthcare company find an ad agency. We sent out 25 Requests for Proposals (RFP). Only three agencies declined to pitch so that left us with 22 candidates who presented a written proposal.

My healthcare company client had five people on their Search Committee. We asked each to review the 22 written proposals and select their favorite three agencies. The three agencies with the most votes would then be the finalists. Only one agency appeared on everyone's list. Why? Because only one ad agency specialized in healthcare. In other words, they were the St. Bernard competing against mixed breeds.

That specialist agency's healthcare client list was longer than everybody else's. Their personnel had significant healthcare experience. The brochure they included in the RFP spoke specifically about their experience in healthcare. On the other hand, the generalist agencies' brochures only talked about themselves. They couldn't justify the cost of a separate brochure for every industry they had experience in.

Getting on the short list

Being a specialist alone didn't get that agency the business but it immediately put the St. Bernard on the short list against 21 competing agencies. What's more, their written RFP pretty much wrote itself. You can bet it didn't take evenings and weekends to put their proposal together because they already knew what to say.

I learned a lot about how sales messages resonate while offering the agency search service. For two years I was listed as an approved agency search consultant by the American Association of Advertising Agencies. In the first year, 99 advertising agencies from throughout America sent me their presentation materials.

They hoped I might have a client that wanted what they had to offer. About 80 of them were generalists and I didn't even know what category or categories to file them under. Even if they were qualified for my future searches, they were harder to find when I began to search my files for experienced candidates. On the other hand, the specialists were easy to find.

TAKEAWAY POINT:

Selling is simply easier when you're a specialist because you have a competitive edge. It's fun being the Alpha dog.

Chapter Five
Specialists Market More Cost-Effectively.

Specialists Market More Cost-Effectively.

It is amazing how costly and inefficient business development is when you don't have a position based on something like specialization. Much more costly! The differences are as pronounced as the contours of a Shar-Pei when comparing generalists and specialists. Using the New Business Balance Wheel on the next page we'll compare specialists and generalists on business development. The five primary components of a business development plan are:

1. Positioning
2. Prospect identification
3. Prospect list management
4. Self promotion
5. Sales tools

The last three spokes are blank because they change by industry.

New Business Balance Wheel

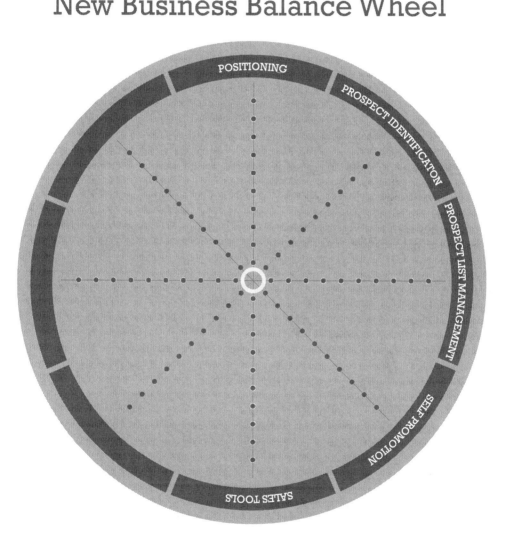

Positioning:

Can you afford to look like the mutt at the pound? There is an extreme emphasis on branding today, but branding is little more than a graphics program if it isn't based on positioning. Just about every dog at the pound is cute, so being cute is not really a good way to position your company.

Positioning is where every business needs to start. Being a specialist is not the only way to position a business, but for this comparison we'll simply look at specialist versus generalist. In the end, you'll see why you want to be a St. Bernard in your industry.

There are several things you need to think about when developing your specialist position.

1. What do my customers and clients really want and need? Is there an opportunity to create a unique new category?

2. What is a position that none of my competitors own that allows me to be the Alpha dog, the leader of the pack?

3. If I could win a significant share of that specialized segment would it alone be enough to support my expense base and growth plans?

It's not a simple process. But it's costly if you don't do it. You can usually start by seeing where your income currently comes from, what you feel you're very good at and what you really like to do. Researching the opportunities is easier than ever thanks to internet services like Google and Bing. One of the biggest reasons to get your specialist position right is that it adds efficiency and cost-effectiveness while helping you communicate.

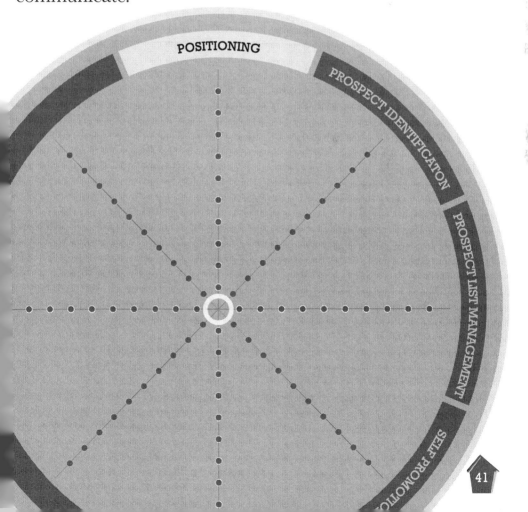

Prospect Identification:
Who are you going to call on?

If you're a generalist, without a specific position, then your prospect list is going to be long and take forever to compile. That's because your market is EVERYBODY. You're better off with quality over quantity and specialization will help you define who your market really is.

In the Introduction I wrote about the St. Bernard pitching his Crossing-the-Alps services to European traders. Perhaps his prospect development would go beyond European traders and include monks and international diplomats. But the litmus test as to whether someone was on his prospect list would be whether or not they needed to travel over the Alps between Switzerland and Italy. If not, they'd be excluded from the list.

With your specialist position your list development should be just as black and white. If you're selling in-line skates, you probably are not going to target the AARP membership list. If you're selling products to hospitals, no need to have banks on your prospect list unless they are third party influencers.

If your product is specific to poodles you don't need a list of Miniature Schnauzer owners.

That decision tree becomes simple when you're working from a pre-identified specialist position.

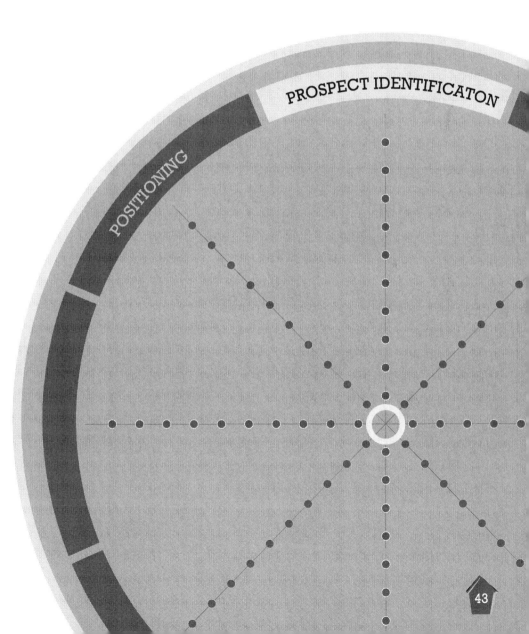

Prospect List Management:

Is it even possible to manage?

If your prospect list does not reflect your specialist position, it is so large and unwieldy that you don't know where to begin. When you decide to mail to the whole list, you'll likely find printing and postage costs alone will blow your budget. A good CRM system can allow you to segment further and reduce some of the cost. But if you can't justify communicating with some of the prospects on your list, why are they on your list in the first place? When you have defined your specialist position and fine tuned your prospect list to support that position, managing your list is doable and affordable.

Referring back to the St. Bernard Crossing the Alps business example, the prospect list should be very user friendly because it only includes prospects that truly have need for your product or service.

PROSPECT LIST MANAGEMENT

PROSPECT IDENTIFICATON

POSITIONING

45

Self Promotion.

What are your networking and public
relations tactics?

The generalist needs to join every club and every
organization because everyone is a prospect. With a
narrower focus, the specialist has fewer groups that are
important and can spend more time with them. If the
service you're selling helps people get across the Alps you
may want to join the European Traders Association (ETA)
and forget about the Egyptian Chamber of Commerce.
That focus will allow you to be more active in the
ETA where you can make a bigger impact by building
relationships that lead to sales.

And the same efficiency comes into play as you go about
PR and media relations decisions. You target media outlets
that European traders read. It's impossible to be effective
everywhere even if you have unlimited dollars. So you go
where your time and money make the most sense. With
your specialist position defined you will have no questions
about what groups and associations you want to join or
what media outlets you want to target. Even your social
media strategies will be more targeted.

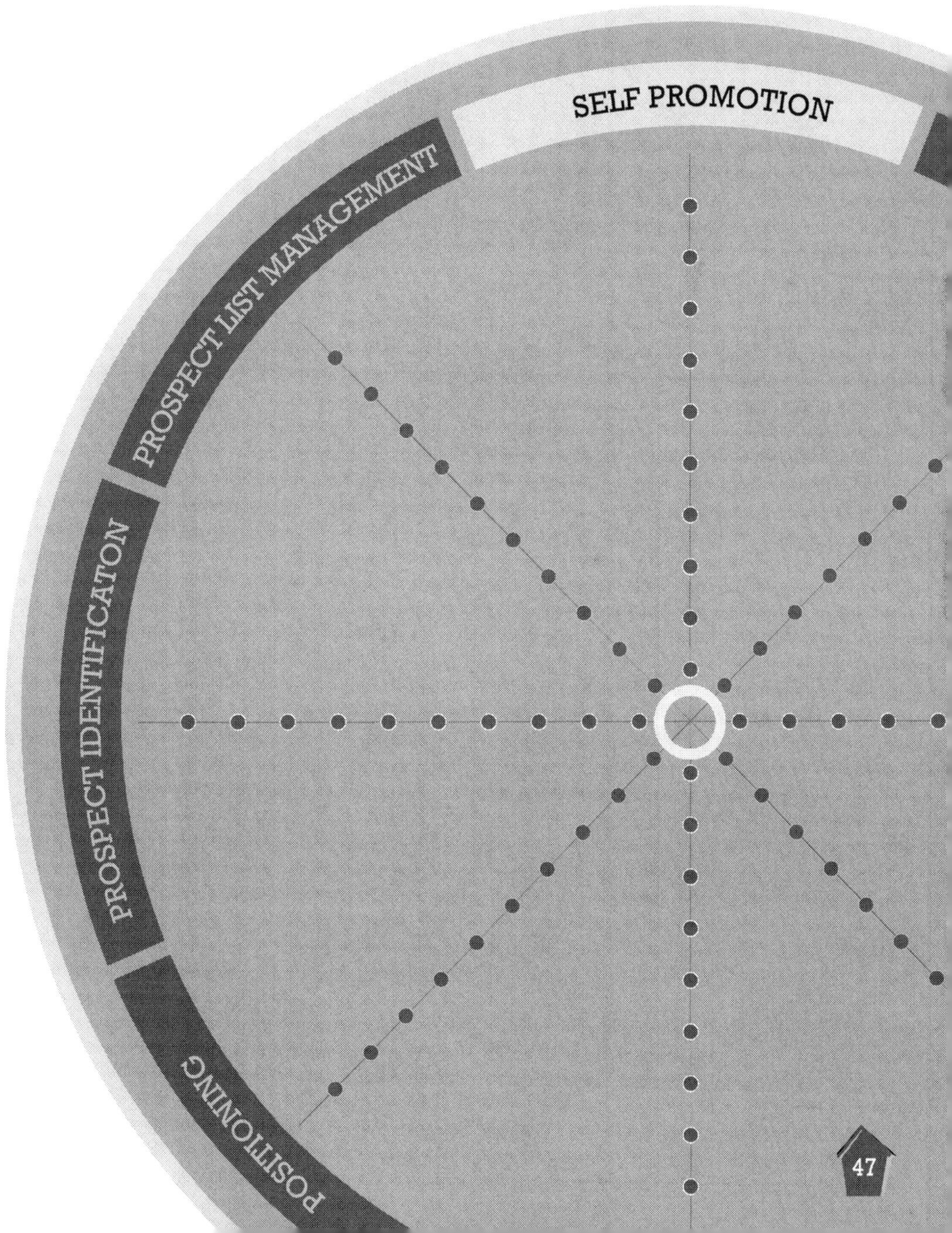
SELF PROMOTION
PROSPECT LIST MANAGEMENT
PROSPECT IDENTIFICATON
POSITIONING

Sales Tools.

How do you make a single website or brochure effective?

Simply put, if you're a generalist you can't. When your audience is broad your messages have to be general. That's what generalists do and it's less effective and more costly. Don't expect a lot of second visits to your website if it's simply full of generalizations. And your expensive new brochure is likely to find the circular file before it finds a file drawer. Websites, brochures and all your other selling tools will have more focus once you know who your specialist position attracts. Knowing your target makes for a better use of your promotional budget.

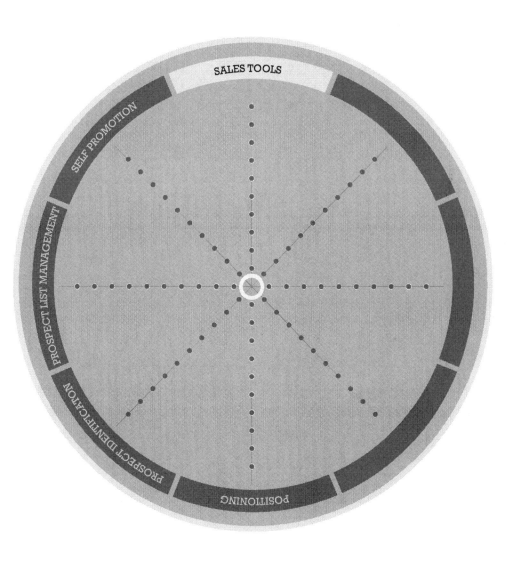

A Gift for You

You can evaluate how you're doing against these criteria and more in a tool I've developed called the New Business Balance Wheel™. A copy is included in the Appendix. Many of my clients use it regularly to measure and fine-tune their business development plan. In this chapter we used the Wheel to put the first five spokes into perspective. Those five apply to every business. The last three can vary depending on how you sell in your buisness. Frequently those spokes relate to presenting and here are some thoughts on that.

Written/Live Presentations.

Can you get away with one good one?

If you're a generalist who considers everyone a prospect you can create one presentation but it won't be powerful. The trouble is, a presentation directed to everybody has to talk about you and not the customer. Talking about "you" rarely works in a selling situation. So you end up doing a new presentation every time you present to a new prospect. Now that's costly and it's usually where mistakes occur! On the other hand, specialists have a concise, easy-to-understand story that is simple to communicate. Even more important, it is easy to understand.

TAKEAWAY POINT:
Being a generalist is a very costly and ineffective way to utilize selling time and marketing dollars.

Chapter Six
Specialists Win at Home and Away.

Specialists Win at Home and Away.

Specialists are able to expand geography and that opens up sales opportunities. That's how you become a big dog. In my hometown of Kansas City, the largest architectural firm specializes in sports arenas and stadiums. The largest advertising firm specializes in digital media. The largest law firm built its practice by specializing in tobacco litigation. The common denominator is specialization.

In each case, the majority of their business is not even in Kansas City. As specialists they've positioned themselves in ways that allow them to export their products and services beyond their geographic center. That's a big reason why a St. Bernard in any industry tends to be larger than their generalist competitors in the same market.

Exporting stadiums.
Think about it. If you're in Minnesota and need an office building there are plenty of architects in Minneapolis/St. Paul that could design you one. But when the Minnesota Twins needed a new baseball stadium, they came to architects in Kansas City who specialize in stadiums. No surprise really.

"As specialists they've positioned themselves in ways that allow them to export their products and services beyond their geographic center"

The New York Yankees, Baltimore Orioles, Chicago White Sox, Cleveland Indians, New York Mets, San Francisco Giants, St. Louis Cardinals and many others did the same thing. And every one of those cities has plenty of local architects.

Meanwhile Kansas City architects without a specialty are fighting it out for strip shopping centers, low rise office buildings and interior finishes. And they're not likely to get a call from Minnesota asking them to do a strip center because the Twin Cities have plenty of talented local architects who can fill those needs.

It's just a fact of life that companies without a position have to work harder for new business. One reason is that they are battling for business in a smaller geography against a larger pool of competitors.

the
ST. BERNARD
PRINCIPLE

You may not be interested in doing business out of your own local area and that's your business decision. There's nothing wrong with that decision.

But if you do want to expand your geographical reach, being a St. Bernard is one way to do it successfully. And specialization can help you win more business even if you never leave your city.

TAKEAWAY POINT:
If you want to open up your geographic opportunities you want to be a St. Bernard.

Chapter Seven
Transitioning from Generalist to Specialist.

Transitioning from Generalist to Specialist.

You might argue that if being a specialist is so appealing, everyone would be doing it.

There are two reasons they don't:
- They fear a specialist position will limit revenues.
- They don't know what to do with their current clients that are outside of that specialty definition.

Effect on revenues

As my friend, Karl Yehle, and I presented a workshop on positioning at an American Marketing Association event, we got a question about specialization that spoke to the first bullet above.

A home remodeling contractor made this statement: "I do all kinds of remodeling projects and don't see how I could afford to focus on just one."

But why not?

I asked him what he liked doing best. He said he really liked doing kitchen remodeling and felt his company was very good at it. To me, that spoke volumes.

When you love to do something and are good at it, you're well on your way to succeeding. I suspect in any city there are enough kitchens being remodeled in any one year that you could make a living doing nothing else. The trick is, getting a higher percentage of kitchen remodeling work to offset lost revenues from bathroom and deck work you might not get.

Assuming the kitchen remodeling market dollars are large enough, there's no reason you can't increase your kitchen market share. If you are positioned in the consumer's mind as the leading kitchen remodeler then your chances of getting a lot more of that business are high. There is available industry market share data from the Joint Center for Housing Studies of Harvard University that would allow you to assess the market potential. The contractor would want to look at that and similar data before committing to that specialist strategy, but if the market volume is there, go for it.

If you don't think it's possible to gain significantly more market share as a specialist, go back and review the first six chapters of this book. It will provide you abundant reasons for you to become a St. Bernard.

Effect on existing clients

So what about the second bullet at the beginning of this chapter? There is no rule that you have to drop all of your other clients if you become a specialist. Accepting repeat business from old clients or transom business that falls into your lap but is outside your specialty is perfectly fine. You simply don't spend a lot of time and money pursuing that work or talking about it.

TAKEAWAY POINT:
Moving from generalist to specialist doesn't have to happen all at once.

Chapter Eight
Living Your Position.

Living Your Position.

Whether you transition into becoming a St. Bernard or jump in with both feet from the start, you need to live your position. That means everything you do from advertising taglines to delivery of your product or service needs to reinforce your specialist position.

A good example is Hallmark Cards. "From 1910 until his death in 1982, J.C. Hall labored tirelessly at making his company synonymous with quality."
That quote is from the book jacket for "When You Care Enough" which was written by Joyce C. Hall with Curtiss Anderson.

That title of course is reflected in the advertising tagline that dates back to 1944, "When You Care Enough to Send the Very Best." In the book, Hall writes "While we thought we had only established a good advertising

"Creativity and quality – in our products, services and all that we do – are essential to success"
                                            - Donald J. Hall

slogan, we soon found out we had made a business commitment as well." His son, Hallmark Chairman Donald J. Hall, formalized that thought when decades later he led development of a "Beliefs and Values" statement that included these words: "Creativity and quality – in our products, services and all that we do – are essential to success" and "We value and are committed to excellence in all we do."

So for Hallmark, their quality position goes beyond advertising slogans to be incorporated into their daily operations. Anything that doesn't support the promise of creativity, quality and excellence in all they do calls the company position into question and has the potential to damage the brand. Hallmark understands that.

So everything Hallmark does is done to keep that quality perception alive. They live it every day in actions large and small. For example, they have precise standards for everything from the reproduction of color on their products and the kind of paper they use, to the flavor of the glue on their envelopes – a secret recipe!

Hallmark's attention to detail is obvious to the consumer when compared with others in their industry. Most companies undersize the back panel of their cards so the front panel overlaps it. Hallmark's back panel, however, is only .003 inch shorter than the front panel. The competition accepts up to a 1/16th (.0625) overlap. Because Hallmark's back panel is tighter to the front cover, it has a craftsman-like finished look. They are able to accomplish this through proprietary templates they have created. What's more, they cut the scores on large presses instead of creasing them. That helps ensure precision in the fold to achieve the slightest offset.

Another example is how Hallmark shoots for a perfect register when applying each process. To achieve this, they have built in predictable tolerance allowances for bleed and line width minimums. That enables them to achieve a perfect register across all of their processes

"If the St. Bernard claims to be the #1 Crossing-the-Alps company, he needs to pay that off. He needs to live it."

which translates into a superb level of quality.
In fact, Hallmark can guarantee a 1/16th inch or less
variation between any processes, even when marrying
processes as different as litho and foil. Typically the
variation is below 1/32nd inch. Their tolerances might
be even less but they have to allow for sheet shrink on
the large presses.

That's what I mean by living your position.

What's that mean to you?
Remember, this book is not about large corporations
like Hallmark but it is about how they got to be large
and profitable. Hallmark Cards understood even in
1944 that you don't just own a position by saying you
own it. You need to deliver on that positioning promise
every day in every way.

If the St. Bernard claims to be the #1 Crossing-the-
Alps company, he needs to pay that off. He needs to live
it. It might mean having to purchase dog sleds and hire
Huskies if that's what it takes to back his promise.

The point is, if you say you are one thing but your actions suggest something else you have lost your edge. You can't say you're a St. Bernard but act like a Beagle. Beagles are fine dogs, but if you say you're a St. Bernard you have to act like one. Customers are becoming more and more turned off by inflated promises. Whereas in the past they saw these exaggerations as just that, today they are viewing them as deceptive and taking them personal.

TAKEAWAY POINT:
There is little room for compromise in paying off your specialist position.

Chapter Nine
How Do You Know if Your Audience Gets It?

How Do You Know if Your Audience Gets It?

If you have an existing product or service your customers and prospects already have you positioned in their minds. The reality is, if you're not positioning yourself, somebody has been choosing a position for you. It might be a customer or a competitor, but someone is positioning you. And it may not be a position you want.

For example, we use airlines as the subject of a positioning exercise we utilize in our workshops and seminars. We ask participants what word or two they associate with five or six airlines. The word consistently associated with US Airways in this exercise is "bankrupt." That's the position they own in the consumer's consciousness (at least the consumers in our workshops). That's the problem with letting someone else establish your position.

What we also found in doing this word association exercise is that the airlines that do a good job of promoting a position have consistent words associated with them. The companies who don't do much to promote a position tend to have many different words associated with them. The latter have no clear picture

> ## "What one or two words would your customers and prospects use to describe your business or product?"

in the consumer's mind. That's better than the US Airways situation but still not good.

Our word association exercise had two airlines coming out positive. The words consistently associated with Southwest Airlines were "cheap fares" and "fun." Words associated with Midwest Airlines (since merged with Frontier Airlines) were also consistent—"4-across seating" and "fresh cookies." Cookies may not sound like a position but it clearly and symbolically reflects people's view of the special treatment and quality they associate with Midwest Airlines.

What one or two words would your customers and prospects use to describe your business or product? What's your current position in your marketplace? Do they see you as a St. Bernard, a Collie or a junk yard dog? Ideally to answer that question you would engage in expensive proprietary research. But if that's not in your budget, you can at least get a hint by using the word association technique we use on the next page.

Research on the cheap

Here are the specifics of how you can develop this word-association research.

Instructions

1. Fill in your company name on the first line.

2. On lines 2, 3 and 4 write the names of your three primary competitors.

3. Next to your company name write the two words that you most identify with your company or product. Then do the same thing next to each of the competitors you've listed.

4. Then ask your employees to do it - include anyone in this exercise who has client or prospect contact including customer service, order takers and sales people.

5. Then ask your clients to do the same thing. It takes them very little time to do this and it can be done with a simple email.

6. Finally, if you have some prospects that would be willing to play along, ask them too.

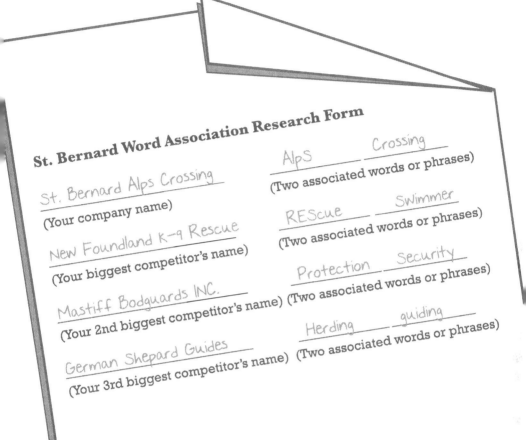

St. Bernard Word Association Research Form

St. Bernard Alps Crossing
(Your company name)

New Foundland K-9 Rescue
(Your biggest competitor's name)

Mastiff Bodguards INC.
(Your 2nd biggest competitor's name)

German Shepard Guides
(Your 3rd biggest competitor's name)

Alps   Crossing
(Two associated words or phrases)

REScue   Swimmer
(Two associated words or phrases)

Protection   Security
(Two associated words or phrases)

Herding   guiding
(Two associated words or phrases)

Once you have all this data collected, review the answers like we just did on the airline quiz.
Ask yourself questions like:

- Do the same words come up frequently when identifying our company or product or are the answers all over the place? Remember, if you have a clear position in the marketplace you probably won't have a lot of different answers.

- How do our competitors measure up to these criteria?

- Do our answers mirror those of clients and prospects? If not, what are our subsequent marketing steps? Do we need to work at changing their impressions? Or are we better off accepting how we're perceived in the marketplace and capitalize by building our marketing messaging around it?

TAKEAWAY POINT:
The best way to find out your current position is to ask.

Chapter Ten
How Are Others
Doing It?

How Are Others Doing It?

Maybe seeing how others have chosen a specialist position will help you figure out how you might do it in your own business. Some of these companies listed below are my clients but most aren't. Still, like me you learn a lot from them from afar via the Internet. Here are a few examples and they are all St. Bernards at some level. The levels are outlined in Chapter Eleven.

Wigged Out

When Tina Herold was diagnosed with breast cancer at 34 years old her husband and children went with her to look for wigs. After trying on several less than fashionable mops she began to cry because of the lack of good choices for young women. As a result, after her chemotherapy, she began her own wig company called Wigged Out. She specializes in an unmet need. Learn more at **www.imwiggedout.com**

SunRun Inc.

Solar power is gaining a lot of press in recent years but how does a company capitalize on the buzz? Well SunRun is literally taking solar power door to door as a specialist in solar power for individual homes. Homeowners can upgrade to solar power for little or no cost. In the category of "residential solar financing" SunRun is the leader with more than 5,000 customers in Arizona, California, Colorado, Massachusetts, New Jersey and Pennsylvania. Take a look at **www.sunrunhome.com**

Decision Graphix
Brad Burrow has a nationally respected animation and video company called Real Media that specializes in production of in-game entertainment for the NCAA, NFL, MLB, NBA, NHL and other sports organizations. In the process of their primary work they began to provide high-end persuasive graphics for litigation attorneys. Rather than try to serve two masters as Real Media, he began a second company. See **www.decisiongraphix.com**

Cordell & Cordell
It's not unusual for attorneys to have a specialty so for Cordell & Cordell to focus on divorce is not news. But their decision to take their specialty to an even narrower position, representing men only, is what makes them a St. Bernard. I hear their radio commercials all the time and they almost make me want to get divorced (but I kind of like my wife). You can see how they build on their position at **www.cordellcordell.com**

Bob's Red Mill

Bob's Red Mill is the nation's leader in stone milling whole grains producing natural foods in the natural way.

Their specialty was producing deep-down, fundamental whole grains. According to an article in *Inc.* magazine, that focus paid off in 1990 when they attended a food trades show in Anaheim and the demand for their products took off as you can see at **www.bobsredmill.com**

Everyscape Inc.

Mok Oh began this Massachusetts' business planning to do photo-realistic 3D tours of streetscapes which put the company head-to-head with Google Street View. Probably not the best idea. So Everyscape made the strategic decision to specialize in business interiors and doubled their size. Take a tour at **www.everyscape.com**

TwelveX

It doesn't matter how much money non-profits raise, most of them are still faced with erratic cash flow.

Brandon Schmidt and Jackson Davis realized that makes the monthly giving concept highly desirable in the erratic cash flow world of non-profits. When they discovered nobody was really specializing in this niche they began TwelveX. In the process, they created a whole new category they call Monthly Engaged Giving. Learn more about this text book piece of positioning at **www.TwelveXGiving.com**

TAKEAWAY POINT:
St. Bernard opportunities occur in many different industries and are only limited by imagination.

Chapter Eleven

No Guts, No Glory.

No Guts, No Glory.

Now's the time to decide if you want to have the impact and status of a Purebred St. Bernard or something less than the best. It's a good time to make that choice from the following options:

Rating	St. Bernard Levels
🦴🦴🦴🦴	**Purebred** – Totally committed to a specialist position
🦴🦴🦴	**Litter Twins** – One dog separated after weaning
🦴🦴	**Rescue Pup** – Second dog shares a doghouse
🦴	**Mixed Breed** – No specialists in the dog pound

The following descriptions will help you flesh out your options as you make your decision:

Level 1. Purebred
After identifying your specialty and determining there is enough business for it to be sustainable, you go all out to become a St. Bernard. That means totally focusing on your specialty and walking away from anything that

doesn't fit the category definition. Obviously this is easier for a start-up but in many cases it can be an easy transition for an existing business that sees opportunity. That means one website, one sales pitch and one mission.

Back in Chapter Seven you read about the remodeling contractor who did all kinds of remodeling and felt he couldn't walk away from everything but kitchens. He said that even in light of the fact that he was passionate about the kitchen work and was exceptionally good at it. By my estimate the kitchen remodeling market was a large enough economic engine to support a kitchen specialist in Kansas City.

As I was recently re-reading *Good To Great* by Jim Collins I was drawn to "The Hedgehog Concept" again and thought about how it applied to this remodeling contractor. The overlapping circles of "The Hedgehog Concept" are:

1. What you are deeply passionate about,

2. What you can be the best in the world at, and

3. What drives your economic engine.

In other words, if the remodeling contractor was passionate about kitchens, best at it, and the income potential was there, why not go for it?

A good example of a purebred company was the one mentioned in Chapter Three that specialized in newsletters. As you'll recall they actually walked away from non-newsletter business rather than risk compromising their specialist position.

A Purebred is so committed to its specialty that customers and prospects have no doubts about whether it is a specialist or someone just claiming to be. Like a Purebred St. Bernard they have the papers to prove who they are and what they're all about. They are certifiably special.

In the Crossing-the-Alps example, because the St. Bernard was totally focused on helping traders cross the Alps, nobody could understand the subtleties like him. Nobody was better equipped to deliver on his specialization promise. Finally, nobody was more believable.

Level 2. Litter Twins

In the canine world there is such a thing as Litter Twins but most breeders don't recommend that they be raised together. That advice could be extended to businesses with multiple significant product groups or services. If you have a strong product group or service that's probably not performing to its fullest potential, you may want to separate it from its siblings after weaning.

In the case of the St. Bernard Crossing-the-Alps Company you wouldn't try to market your St. Bernard Guard Service as part of the other company. At least not if you thought it could be significant on its own. You would separate the siblings to demonstrate your commitment to each one. Your messaging would be totally different for the second one. The St. Bernard Guard Service could mention their relationship with the Crossing-the-Alps Company but wouldn't dwell on it. The new Guard Service sister company will be more convincing and profitable by functioning away from its sibling.

To follow the Litter Twin strategy you would start a division, a subsidiary or whatever you want to call it. You'd need a separate website, sales pitch and mission as you create a parallel business universe.

It would have a separate budget cost-effectively targeted to that specialty's unique audience and industry.

Decision Graphix that was mentioned in the Chapter Ten is a good example of a Litter Twins company who removed a successful service from their primary company to make it stronger. They saw a growing opportunity to provide high-end persuasive graphics to litigation attorneys and gave that part of their business its own home.

You can own a Black Labrador and a Golden Retriever at the same time, but just don't take them on the same hunting expedition.

Level 3: Rescue Pup

Some companies have a high-performing product or service group that is lost in anonymity within the structure of the company as a whole. That being said, the parent company is not willing to break that group off with a separate identity. They know it's inexpensive today to develop a second website and sales literature for a specialized service but choose not to do it.

That being said, you can implement a Rescue Pup strategy and give the high-potential group a revered position within your existing marketing structure. For example, you might make your star specialty a feature part of your web home page. Then link it to a specialist page or pages. In other words, you don't create a separate website but you do feature this specialty prominently on your existing corporate website.

This is low risk, low reward. You announce this specialty area but it is still secondary to the overall thrust of your company. You're part St. Bernard and part pound dog. You commit a little more sales time to your specialty area but don't get aggressive until you see it working. In essence, you rescue that product group or service from the anonymity that it experiences when treated equally with everything else your company offers.

By giving that strong product group or service a little heavier play, it may enjoy more success. But if it is really loaded with sales and profit potential you might want to seriously consider the Litter Twin approach.

Level 4: Mixed Breed

Maybe you're content to be a generalist. A Mixed Breed is what you are and it seems to be working for you. Your company looks a little like a dog pound where there are all kinds of dogs that are hoping to get noticed before they end up in the big doghouse in the sky. It's a conscious decision on your part. But you're probably not maximizing your potential.

Perhaps you're holding back because you simply can't identify a specialist opportunity. If that's the case you might want to be prepared to sniff out opportunities like a Black and Tan Coonhound would. One thing for sure, you're not going to have the upside you could have as a St. Bernard. Good luck finding selling points to launch a Crossing-the-Alps service.

Even if you decide not to become a St. Bernard, you'll learn a lot about your business by just considering how being one might work for you. Once you begin studying the principle of specialization you will be surprised how many successful St. Bernard businesses you see in your daily activities. When a St. Bernard comes into your yard, it's a beautiful thing to watch. He engages with his personality and flexes his muscles for great success.

TAKEAWAY POINT:
There's never been a better time to
decide whether you can be a
St. Bernard.

Appendix

To break down the elements that lead up to a sale I developed a business development self evaluation tool. It's called the New Business Balance Wheel.™ Many seminar participants tell me this tool has been really helpful in recognizing their strengths and shortcomings. The Wheel includes eight spokes, five of which apply to every business and are so labeled. Spoke descriptions for the final three spokes are blank to allow you to tailor the Wheel to your business situation. Make a photo copy of this page, fill in the blanks and follow the instructions at the bottom of the Wheel.

Before completing the evaluation, fill in a label for each of the three blank spokes based on what is relevant to your specific industry. For example, for a professional services company the additional spokes might be Written Presentations, Live Presentations, and Post-Pitch Follow-Up. For a residential remodeler they might be Remodeling Shows, Advertising, and Customer Referral Program.

I encourage you to use the New Business Balance Wheel and go through the exercise of completing it two or three times a year to measure your progress. You may even want to have several members of management complete it to see if everyone's perceptions are in sync. It's important for everyone to be on the same page.

New Business Balance Wheel

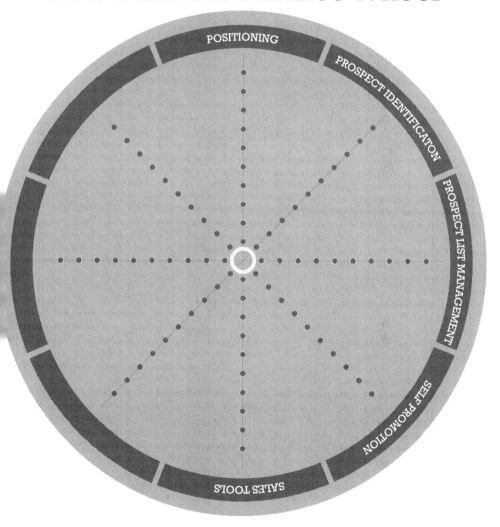

Rate each phase of your new business effort on a scale
from 1-10 (with 10 being the outside edge of the wheel)
by filling in the circle at the appropriate point along
each line. Once you've rated each line,
connect the dots!

Index

Index continued

About the Author
Paul J. Welsh

During his career, Welsh has held management positions in corporations, publishing companies and advertising agencies.

He has founded or co-founded six businesses. One business he co-founded started from scratch and employed 75 people when he sold to his partners. Three of the six businesses remain in existence and only one went belly up. The latter taught Welsh that you learn from your time as a mutt as well as being a St. Bernard. When you go belly up you can't wait around for someone to scratch your tummy.

Welsh has been an advocate for small business and entrepreneurism since 1979, almost two years before co-founding his first business. That was his focus when he served on the Board of the Greater Kansas City Chamber of Commerce. He served on the Small Business Public Relations Committee and chaired Small Business Brain Exchange.

Welsh was a founding Board member of the Metropolitan Entrepreneurs Council with people like Neil Patterson, co-founder of Cerner, and Marvin Manlove, a founding principal 360 Architecture. Welsh has testified before state legislatures on small business issues.

His advertising writing work has been recognized nationally and internationally with awards from CLIO, New York Ad Club, New York Art Directors Club, The One Show, Print Magazine, Communications Arts, Magazine Publishers Association Objectives & Results, the National Agri-Marketing Association among others.

He was named AAF-Kansas City 2001 Advertising Executive of the Year.

In the past he has served as an adjunct professor in marketing communications at Avila University, The Art Institutes International and has mentored many collegians in various scholarship programs.

For speaking engagements or consultation, Paul Welsh can reached at **pwelsh@WelshWrites.com**

Made in the USA
San Bernardino, CA
25 November 2019

60433475R00071